Mrs Meadowsweet

A Play

David Campton

FOR AMATEUR PRODUCTION ENQUIRIES

UNITED KINGDOM AND WORLD
EXCLUDING NORTH AMERICA
plays@SamuelFrench-London.co.uk
020 7255 4302/01

Each title is subject to availability from Samuel French,

depending upon country of performance.

CHARACTERS

Miss Jerrold
Miss Brazenose
Fleur
Alice
Mrs Meadowsweet
Inga

The action takes place in the lounge of a small country guest house in the West Country

Time—the present

During the play the Lights dim to denote passages of time

AUTHOR'S NOTE

Although for the purposes of this script *Respite* is set in the West Country, there is no reason why the action should not take place in any other country district—as long as Mrs Meadowsweet's accent is changed accordingly.

MRS MEADOWSWEET*

The lounge at "Respite", a small country guest house in the West Country

It is late afternoon in summer

The lounge contains several easy chairs (with perhaps a settee) arranged around the room—one at least has its back to the audience. Near the chairs are low tables on which afternoon tea has been served. This is nearly over but tea-things have yet to be cleared from some of the tables. There is an archway to the entrance hall at the rear and french windows opening to the garden at one side

As the CURTAIN *rises, Miss Brazenose, an upright person in late middle age, is gazing through the french windows whilst Miss Jerrold, an older silver-haired lady, smiles happily to herself. For a while neither says anything, then Miss Jerrold starts to make a pronouncement*

Miss Jerrold Tea is . . .

There is a pause until Miss Brazenose realizes she has been spoken to

Miss Brazenose (*at last*) Yes?

Another pause while Miss Jerrold sorts this out

Miss Jerrold Yes?
Miss Brazenose You said "Tea. Is."
Miss Jerrold Did I . . .? I must have been about to say—er . . .
Miss Brazenose Yes?
Miss Jerrold I've forgotten.
Miss Brazenose Something about tea?
Miss Jerrold A passing reflection. (*She thinks*) It appears to have passed.
Miss Brazenose (*trying to work it out*) Tea is—what?

---

*N.B. Paragraph 3 on page ii of this Acting Edition regarding photocopying and video-recording should be carefully read.

Miss Jerrold A soothing influence?
Miss Brazenose Is that what you were going to say?
Miss Jerrold I've no idea why. Who needs soothing?
Miss Brazenose The fruit cake was awfully good.
Miss Jerrold After tea one feels so at peace with—with ...
Miss Brazenose Is *that* what you were going to say?
Miss Jerrold Who knows? At peace with ...

A distant door is slammed. This is followed by raised and angry voices approaching

Fleur (*off*) If you can't speak without being abusive, you might as well shut up.
Alice (*off*) I only asked where the hell we were.
Fleur (*off*) You ought to know. You were driving.
Alice (*off*) You were supposed to be reading the map.

The speakers pause by the archway. They are Alice Benson, a hard-faced person in her early forties and her younger sister, Fleur, slighter and more accommodating but no less hard-hitting when crossed

Fleur How could I read anything with you swerving all over the place?
Alice I kept swerving because the road bends like that—if a God-forsaken cart track can be called a road.

They observe the room and its occupants

H'm. Ah. Can we eat here?
Miss Jerrold This is *Respite*.
Alice What sort of answer's that?
Fleur We are looking for a place to sleep, too.
Miss Brazenose You'll need to ask Mrs Meadowsweet.
Miss Jerrold But I'm sure there'll be a room. There always is.
Alice One thing at a time. I haven't mentioned a room.
Miss Jerrold Tea's nearly over, but not to worry. Nobody worries here. Would you like to sit by the window? For the scent from the garden, you know. And, of course, one sees so much more from here. I'm Miss Jerrold. And you are?
Alice Benson. Alice. Miss. If we're name swapping, this is my sister. Fleur. Harris. Divorced. Any other titbits you'd like from the data bank?

Fleur You'll have to forgive my sister, Miss Jerrold. She's not always so uncouth. Only when she's trying to embarrass me.

Alice My sister has a talent for rousing the worst in anyone.

Miss Brazenose Don't bicker. Please!

Miss Jerrold Remember they've only just arrived, Miss Brazenose.

Alice Shan't be staying long, either. So if you want to insult me, feel free. I shan't be around to remind you.

Miss Jerrold Can you be so sure?

Alice None surer. I don't know whether it's the place or the people, but something here is giving me the creeps.

Miss Brazenose Everybody at *Respite* is happy. Happy!

Alice I'm not.

Fleur surreptitiously kicks Alice's ankle

(*Gasping, turning to Fleur*) Keep your feet to yourself, dear, or I might break your ankle, kicking back.

Miss Jerrold Mrs Meadowsweet is responsible, of course. A chat with Mrs Meadowsweet can be so reassuring.

Fleur We're on holiday. Just meandering. Taking our chance. We haven't booked anywhere in advance.

Alice Even if we did it wouldn't be right for certain people when we got there.

Fleur Some people find fault with anything.

Alice Meaning me?

Fleur Who else is there as bloody-minded?

Alice Do you want me to tell you?

Miss Brazenose (*vehemently*) Stop it!

Miss Jerrold Why, Miss Brazenose ...

Miss Brazenose I told you. Fighting upsets me.

Alice Who's fighting?

Miss Brazenose Can't you keep your quarrels to yourself without involving bystanders? I must—I must go to Mrs Meadowsweet. At once.

Miss Jerrold Do that, my dear.

Miss Brazenose Snap. Snarl. Like animals. Disgusting ...

Miss Brazenose hurries out through the french windows, complaining to herself

Fleur But Miss ...

Alice Let her go. I'm prepared to skip tea and leave this minute.

Miss Jerrold You're troubled, too, aren't you, Miss Benson?
Alice Me?
Miss Jerrold It shows in little ways. . . . Perhaps I ought to follow Miss Brazenose. These nervous outbursts are so distressing. But if I were you, I'd stay for tea. The scones are very good just now, and the cream cakes are delicious.

Miss Jerrold exits through the french windows

Fleur What must she be thinking of us?
Alice I don't give a damn what any of them think.
Fleur I know you never learned how to behave, but do you want everybody else to know?
Alice If this place turns out to be a disaster, don't blame me. All Devon to choose from and you pick on a Wendy House full of weirdies.
Fleur All right, all right, so you still want to work off your temper. Just give it a rest while I wash and change.

Mrs Meadowsweet, a comfortable person of indeterminate age with a reassuring smile and a strong West Country accent, appears in the archway

Mrs Meadowsweet Terrible dusty these lanes in summer, my dear.
Alice What?

Alice and Fleur, startled, turn to Mrs Meadowsweet

Mrs Meadowsweet You'd like to do something about the dust. There's hot and cold in all rooms.
Fleur Mrs—er—Meadowsweet?
Mrs Meadowsweet Welcome to *Respite* my dears.
Alice How do you expect anybody to find this place? In the middle of nowhere and half a mile from the beaten track.
Mrs Meadowsweet I always say, if you find your way here, you're meant to be here.
Alice What a way to run a business!
Mrs Meadowsweet Or put the other way round, if you weren't meant to be here, you'd never have found us at all.
Fleur We wondered if you . . .
Mrs Meadowsweet There's always a welcome at *Respite*. You'll be wanting a room.
Fleur Yes.

Alice I didn't say "yes". (*She turns abruptly and looks through the windows*)

Fleur I said "yes", Alice. You can please yourself. I'll be staying. Just for tonight.

Mrs Meadowsweet As long as you need, my dear. Stay just as long as you need.

Fleur The cases are in the car.

Mrs Meadowsweet Inga can lend a hand. (*She calls*) Inga ...! You'll be able to see the gardens from your room, my dear.

Alice turns back

All the rooms are named after flowers. Lavender, Wild Thyme, Musk Rose ...

Inga appears in the archway. Younger than the others, there is a suggestion of withdrawal in her attitude—yet she seems quite happy

Ah, Inga. I'm putting these ladies in Honeysuckle.

Fleur Coming up, Alice?

Alice You haven't asked yet how much it's going to cost.

Mrs Meadowsweet No more than you can afford, my dear. I promise.

Fleur (*to Inga*) Come on, then.

Mrs Meadowsweet I hope you find Honeysuckle to your liking. Or did you want separate rooms? There's Comfrey next to Honeysuckle.

Fleur One double will do for me and my sister, thank you.

Fleur and Inga exit

Alice All the better to fight you in.

Mrs Meadowsweet Why don't you sit down, my dear? I'll have tea brought in directly.

Alice H'm. (*As a sort of grudging apology*) This has been a hell of a day.

Mrs Meadowsweet I'm listening.

Alice That was an explanation, not a bid for sympathy.

Mrs Meadowsweet Guests come and go with their problems. They do say I'm a good listener.

Alice There's one of 'em out looking for you now.

Mrs Meadowsweet That's usual. But you're here, my dear. And so am I.

Alice I've never been one to pass on troubles.

Mrs Meadowsweet I understand. You'd rather keep them handy. In the middle of the night, when you can't sleep, there's nothing like a thorny problem for passing the time. You had a bad day, you say.

Alice It really blew up over the ploughman's lunch. That wasn't worth quarrelling over. Not even worth remembering.

Mrs Meadowsweet The ploughman's lunch?

Alice (*the memory of it fading*) The—ploughman's lunch.

Mrs Meadowsweet Well, that's better out than in, isn't it? I always say there's nothing in this world as sour as a memory turned wrong. So why not let me have it?

Alice You?

Mrs Meadowsweet I can't just *take* memories, though. Only accept what is offered. Even the false memories, though we won't talk about them, if you don't mind. Not nice at all.

Alice Exactly what does that mean?

Mrs Meadowsweet I'm often surprised at the way folk will cling to something that must be hurting so much. Like the Spartan boy and the fox. Were you told that story at school? How he let the animal eat his heart out rather than complain. So unnecessary. Especially when there's somebody at hand to take away the pain.

Alice Nobody can do that.

Mrs Meadowsweet You haven't given *Respite* a chance yet, my dear. Now what's on your mind?

Alice Nothing.

Mrs Meadowsweet (*wincing*) Botheration. That's not strictly true.

Alice It sounds better than "get lost".

Mrs Meadowsweet You do enjoy scratching at sores, don't you?

Alice What do you think you are? A sort of social worker?

Mrs Meadowsweet I have the gift, my dear. Others may have it, though I never heard of others. But, having it, shouldn't I use it? I can smooth away troubles better than any liniment.

Alice I tell you I'm in no sort of trouble.

Mrs Meadowsweet (*wincing*) A forgiveable lie. I always say trouble is like an aching tooth. You can put up with it for just so long, then out it has to come.

Alice You'd be surprised.

Mrs Meadowsweet You'll find unburdening comes easier with practice. I never force anyone, of course; but are you sure you don't want to tell me what is wrong between you and your sister?

Alice Between me and Fleur? Nothing.

Mrs Meadowsweet (*wincing*) No insult intended, but sometimes a lie tells more than the truth.

Alice All right, we had a spat. What's new about that? We've been sparring since we were girls.

Mrs Meadowsweet Why?

Alice Does there have to be a reason? Perhaps because I was born first. Perhaps because I had the brains and she had the beauty. It can't all be gone yet—the way men look at her. Even when we were younger they never looked at me at all.

Mrs Meadowsweet Ah. Does it hurt so much now to remember?

Alice Remember? Remember what?

Mrs Meadowsweet When I first saw you I said to myself, "There's a person with a load on her mind."

Alice Then you misinformed yourself.

Mrs Meadowsweet Why can't you forgive her?

Alice Forgive what? Fleur never did me any harm.

Mrs Meadowsweet (*wincing*) Ugh!

Alice You could do with an aspirin, Mrs Meadowsweet.

Mrs Meadowsweet I can do without those false memories, Miss Benson.

Alice Oh?

Mrs Meadowsweet I tell you a false memory is worse than a knife.

Alice Would you be calling me a liar?

Mrs Meadowsweet Exactly why do you dislike your sister, Miss Benson? Just what is it you'd rather not remember?

Alice (*indignantly*) I tell you ... (*She gives a wry laugh*) You're a knowing old devil, Mrs Meadowsweet.

Mrs Meadowsweet I've had experience, my dear.

Alice I don't know why I should tell you. But. ... There was one man. A long time ago. Sir Galahad, Superman and Young Lochinvar rolled into one.

Mrs Meadowsweet In a manner of speaking.

Alice I thought he was interested in me. No—he *was* interested. We went out together—concerts and country walks. But Fleur married him. A couple of years ago they parted—and she turned up again on my doorstep. I think I could have made him happy; but the clock can't be turned back. The waste is what hurts most. Years thrown away.

Mrs Meadowsweet Mmm. Memories can be so painful, my dear. But you're not going to worry about that one any longer, are you? (*Firmly*) I say you're not going to worry.

Alice Worry?

Mrs Meadowsweet Worry.

Alice Worry about what?

Mrs Meadowsweet What you are worrying about.

Alice What *was* I worrying about?

Mrs Meadowsweet Don't you worry, my dear. I always say what you don't remember can't hurt you.

Alice I meant to say I . . . What was I saying?

Mrs Meadowsweet Don't you go chasing after old memories, my dear. Let them go. And if anything else bothers you, I'm always ready to listen.

Alice Not much chance of that. We never stay in any place more than one night.

Mrs Meadowsweet Perhaps you'll make an exception at *Respite*.

Alice That depends on my sister.

Mrs Meadowsweet At any rate you'll rest easier tonight, my dear.

Alice Doesn't that depend on my sister, too?

Mrs Meadowsweet I always say it's difficult to quarrel when you've forgotten what you're quarrelling about.

Alice You don't know my sister.

Fleur enters through the archway

Fleur We've taken your case upstairs. Or would you rather sleep in the open?

Mrs Meadowsweet Back so soon, dear? And I've still to arrange for your tea. I'll have it on the tray in a minute. With cream.

Mrs Meadowsweet bustles out through the archway

Fleur There's one cat who looks as though she's already been at the cream.

Alice Yes?

Fleur What have you got to smile about?

Alice I've been talking to Mrs Herbaceous.

Fleur About me?

Alice Why should we want to talk about you? I can't exactly remember *what* we were talking about.

Fleur That must have been interesting. If you hadn't kept her chattering, tea might have been ready by now.

Alice Sorry.

Fleur What?

Alice I said "sorry". Want to make something of it?

Fleur That's more like your old self. What got into you?

Alice Into me?

Fleur What's happened to the celebrated Benson temper?

Alice Oh, you know how it is.

Fleur Do I?

Alice How can you argue when there's nothing to argue about?

Fleur That's never stopped you before.

Inga enters through the archway with a tray

Inga Tea.

Alice Thank you—Inga, isn't it?

Inga Yes. Inga.

Alice Can we have it on the table by the window?

Inga By the window. (*She takes the tray to the table*)

Alice (*looking through the window*) There's a lovely view from here.

Inga Mrs Meadowsweet said ... She said ...

Fleur Yes?

Inga There's a lovely view.

Alice Lovely gardens. Lovely trees. They make a lovely screen. What is behind the trees?

Fleur The lovely compost heap?

Alice So peaceful here.

Inga Yes. Peaceful. (*She sets the table for tea then collects the used tea-things from the other tables*)

Alice Are you all the staff there is here?

Inga Me?

Alice Do they make you do everything?

Inga I think there is ... There is ... There is more tea if you ring for it.

Alice How long have you been here?

Inga I—I. ... My name is Inga.

Alice What sort of answer's that?

Fleur Well, thank you, Inga.
Inga Dinner is served in the dining-room at half past seven.
Alice Are you cooking that, too?

Inga hurries out with the tray

Fleur A tip doesn't always make up for rudeness, you know.
Alice Rudeness? Was I rude? I'm sorry.
Fleur When you've finished snuffling at that window, we'll sit down to tea.
Alice There's a bed of stocks here.
Fleur All this sweetness and light is leading up to something.
Alice I can't understand why you're in such a bad mood.
Fleur Neat. Oh, very neat. Which makes everything my fault. This afternoon never happened, of course.
Alice This afternoon?
Fleur You know very well. After the ploughman's lunch.
Alice What ploughman's lunch?
Fleur What a convenient memory. *The* ploughman's lunch— wrong bread, wrong cheese, wrong pickle. Remember?
Alice No.
Fleur Give me strength!
Alice If I did remember, I'd probably want to spit in your eye, so it's probably as well I can't.
Fleur But it happened only today. A few hours ago.
Alice Who cares? (*She takes a deep breath*) Pinks, gillyflowers, alyssum. I wonder who looks after the gardens here? Do you really want to move on tomorrow?
Fleur We always have done.
Alice I thought, perhaps, we might stay here for another day.
Fleur I think not. Not in this place.
Alice Let's not argue, dear. We'll discuss it tomorrow. Amicably.
Fleur That'll be the day.
Alice (*sighing*) Ah!
Fleur What's the matter now?
Alice I'm not sure. I feel—somehow—sort of empty. . . . Shall I pour?

The Lights fade to denote the passage of time

Pause. Fleur exits

Lights up

It is teatime, a few days later. Alice is sitting alone, contemplating the tea in front of her

Miss Jerrold enters through the archway

Miss Jerrold Picking up our little ways I see, Miss Benson. Served before any of us today. (*She sits at another table*)
Alice (*offering her a cup*) Would you like to join me?
Miss Jerrold My tray will be along directly. They know my little ways. Is it raspberry jam again?
Alice The gardens are full of fruit.
Miss Jerrold The time of year.
Alice I had a walk round the garden this afternoon.
Miss Jerrold Not a weed in sight.
Alice The vegetable gardens. Asparagus, spinach and all that. Who digs them?
Miss Jerrold I've never been greatly concerned about vegetable gardens. Spinach is all very well in its way, but it can't compare with sweet peas for colour.
Alice One hole was enormous—at least six feet long and very deep. I don't know what's going in there.
Miss Jerrold Celery. Or compost. Isn't your sister having tea?
Alice She's out walking, too. On her own. Said she wants to "work things out for herself"—whatever that means. She's worrying about something.
Miss Jerrold But nobody here worries. Mrs Meadowsweet doesn't approve.
Alice Keeps insisting there's something not right—if only she could put her finger on it.
Miss Jerrold Hasn't she talked to Mrs Meadowsweet?
Alice She talks to other guests. Then *they* go to Mrs Meadowsweet.

Fleur enters through the french windows

Fleur Alice, we are moving on tomorrow. Definitely.
Alice If you say so, dear.
Fleur You said that yesterday.
Alice Did I?
Fleur And the day before. If we stay here much longer, we'll take root.
Miss Jerrold A very pleasant spot to be planted in, Mrs Harris.

Fleur That's all very well for vegetables, Miss Jerrold, but we don't happen to be turnips.

Alice Have you been round the vegetable gardens, dear?

Fleur I don't want to be reminded of my fellow guests. Before we started on this trip we agreed—and it's miracle enough for us to agree on anything—one night in each place. We've been here for three days.

Alice Tomorrow then, dear.

Fleur I'm not even sure we ought to wait so long.

Alice What *is* the matter?

Fleur That's what I want to know.

Miss Brazenose, smiling somewhat vacantly, enters with a tray

Fleur Been to fetch your own, Miss Brazenose?

Miss Brazenose puts the tray down by Miss Jerrold

Miss Jerrold Thank you.

Fleur But you're one of the guests, Miss Brazenose. What do you think you're doing?

Miss Brazenose Me? I'm serving at table.

Fleur But why?

Miss Brazenose Why?

Fleur Where's Inga?

Miss Brazenose Inga?

Fleur Yes, Inga.

Miss Jerrold Who is Inga?

Fleur You know as well as I do, Miss Jerrold. You can't have forgotten her. Inga was waiting at table this morning. And yesterday. And the day before. And making beds and carrying baggage. When there was work to be done, there was Inga doing it. Now here's Miss Brazenose in her place. Miss Brazenose!

Miss Brazenose I'm Miss Brazenose.

Fleur Don't you remember me?

Miss Brazenose Should I?

Fleur You protested enough when we first met. My sister and I were squabbling. You objected. Loudly. You went to Mrs Meadowsweet.

Miss Brazenose I know Mrs Meadowsweet. So understanding.

Miss Jerrold Mrs Meadowsweet is a very remarkable person. Such a comfort.

Fleur Comfort!

Miss Jerrold Only a word. For something that can't exactly be put into words.

Fleur That's true enough. Miss Brazenose . . .

Alice Fleur, dear, have your tea and let the poor woman alone. She's only doing her job.

Fleur It's not her job. It's Inga's job. Don't tell me *you* can't remember Inga either.

Alice I don't want to be drawn into an argument, dear.

Fleur But even if Inga walked out; if Inga were fired; if Inga broke a leg; why is Miss Brazenose taking her place? Miss Brazenose of all people.

Miss Brazenose (*thinking hard*) My name is Emily Brazenose and—and . . .

Alice You're becomine a wee bit hysterical, Fleur. If you carry on that way, you'll have the waitress hysterical, too.

Fleur She—is—not—the waitress. Are you, Miss Brazenose?

Miss Brazenose (*flustered*) Other people are waiting to be served. Here. On the lawn. Everywhere.

Fleur Are you doing this as a favour? For a bet? As a joke?

Miss Brazenose Too many questions.

Fleur Remember who you are.

Miss Brazenose I am—I am . . .

Fleur What you are. Where you came from. What you are doing here. Think.

Miss Brazenose I must talk to Mrs Meadowsweet. Now.

Distressed, Miss Brazenose hurries out through the archway

Alice Why did you have to upset her? She was so happy serving tea.

Fleur The way you're happy.

Alice Am I? I suppose I must be. Contented at any rate. Now do sit down and enjoy your scones.

Fleur I don't like it.

Alice Then order something else. Everybody is most obliging.

Fleur Too obliging. Don't you get the feeling that there's— something missing? What sort of place is this. What have you got to say, Miss Jcrrold?

Miss Jerrold Now you're asking. Let me see. Let's say that since I came here I feel as though I haven't a care in the world. To me

this place seems a sort of Shangri-la. A *Lost Horizon*. Did you
see that old film?

Fleur Are you sure it's only tea you've been drinking?

Miss Jerrold No need for anything more potent. The air here is
like wine. Dandelion. Elderflower ...

Fleur How long have you been here?

Miss Jerrold Me? I ... It's on the tip of my tongue. Must be ...
No, before that. Oh, ask Mrs Meadowsweet. She'll know.

Alice Yes, dear. Have a talk with Mrs Meadowsweet. She'll
straighten you out.

Fleur How? Will she have me serving at table, too? Or would I be
better at digging the garden?

Mrs Meadowsweet enters through the archway

Mrs Meadowsweet I always say everybody is much happier when
they're occupied.

Fleur Is that why you found Miss Brazenose something to do?

Mrs Meadowsweet A kindness, my dear. But we'd both take it as a
kindness on your part if you didn't try to make her remember.
Painful memories are best not put back, Mrs Harris. Don't you
agree?

Fleur I wouldn't know. I don't have any.

Mrs Meadowsweet winces

Headache?

Mrs Meadowsweet An old trouble.

Fleur And who's to cure the doctor? What a pity you can't talk to
yourself.

Mrs Meadowsweet I bear what I have to bear with patience, my
dear. But there's no reason why you should. Now what is
upsetting you?

Fleur Nothing.

Mrs Meadowsweet (*wincing*) That isn't strictly true, is it?

Fleur How do you know?

Mrs Meadowsweet The bigger the lie, the sharper the twinge. Why
are you so concerned about Miss Brazenose?

Fleur I'm not.

Mrs Meadowsweet (*wincing*) Why tell a lie when the truth serves as
well? Are you afraid to confide in me, my dear?

Fleur No.

Mrs Meadowsweet (*wincing*) There's no need. I don't practise
   dark arts. Just a natural cure.
Alice I can't understand why my sister is making such a fuss over
   the waitress.
Miss Jerrold After all, somebody has to serve at table.
Fleur But not her.
Alice What have you got against her? She's quite efficient.
Fleur She's on our side of the counter. Don't you remember?
   Either of you? Miss Jerrold? Alice?

They look blank

Mrs Meadowsweet They spoke to me earlier, dear. Now what
   have *you* got to tell me?
Fleur The day before yesterday Miss Brazenose was sitting next to
   our table—complaining about us like a regular. And why not?
   Paying customers don't expect to find themselves in the middle
   of a dog-fight. But I don't expect to see paying customers
   fetching and carrying.
Mrs Meadowsweet Ah, yes.
Fleur She's been talking to you, hasn't she?
Mrs Meadowsweet Miss Brazenose had some very unhappy
   memories. Locked away deep. So deep and so unhappy whole
   days had to go by before she'd bring just one of them to me. I'm
   afraid they're not all out yet. But you're not bothered by Miss
   Brazenose any longer, are you, my dear? Are you? Not by Miss
   Brazenose.
Fleur Miss Brazenose?
Mrs Meadowsweet The waitress. You were telling me about her.
Fleur Was I?
Mrs Meadowsweet She's waiting in the kitchen for me now and
   rather distressed. But I had to deal with your little problem first.
Fleur My—little problem?
Mrs Meadowsweet We really must have a long chat, my dear.
   Bring all *your* problems to me. Sooner or later everyone does.
   Now don't let your tea get cold.

   Mrs Meadowsweet exits through the archway

Fleur slowly sits

Miss Jerrold The scones are not so good today. And no cream
   cakes. Is the cook losing her touch?

Fleur What—what was I saying?

Alice It's not important, Fleur, dear.

Fleur But it is. It is. Something's missing. I was saying that we must leave tomorrow, and then—and then . . .

Alice Don't ask me to remember for you.

Fleur Was that it? What else don't you remember, Alice?

Alice I can remember everything that I need to remember.

Fleur Can you?

Alice Why, I can remember right back to the time when we were girls—wearing pigtails.

Miss Jerrold How nice.

Fleur Do you remember how I cut yours off?

Alice The parties and picnics. Tea by the river . . .

Fleur The time we fought and kicked the basket into the water? You were the one in disgrace over it.

Alice I don't think I want to remember that.

Fleur You never had any difficulty over your recollections before. You kept a vast store at the ready—like a stock-pile of missiles. You could always produce one or another to back up any disagreement.

Alice Perhaps it's as well I can't think of one now.

Fleur But why can't you? Why?

Miss Jerrold When I was a girl we had a sundial in our garden. On it was written, "I only count your sunny hours."

Fleur Not even—Martin?

Alice Martin who?

Fleur You haven't forgotten him. You couldn't. This is a new game, isn't it? You're playing me up. You think I'm scared and you're trying to make matters worse.

Alice Me? Why are you pretending to remember things that I can't?

Miss Jerrold There's no fruit cake today either.

Fleur Did you talk to Mrs Meadowsweet about Martin?

Alice How can I talk to anybody about somebody I never knew?

Miss Jerrold And I really must mention the sandwiches.

Fleur Alice, I took him from you. At least that's what you accused me of. The night we announced the engagement you . . . I needed ten stitches afterwards. The scar's still there. Do you want to see?

Alice No.

Fleur Then you do remember.
Alice No.
Fleur What are you trying to do to me? After the divorce you had your chance to gloat. And you gloated.
Alice Did I?
Fleur When I came crawling back for the sake of a roof over my head.
Alice Did you?
Fleur You can't sit there like a lumpy mattress pretending those hassles meant nothing to you.
Alice Did they?
Fleur This is a new way of twisting the knife, isn't it? Because if it isn't, I'm not scared any longer. I'm terrified.
Alice Fleur, dear, we're sisters. I'm sure of that at any rate.
Fleur Yes, Alice. We are sisters.
Alice Would sisters do such things to each other?
Fleur What is this place doing to you?
Miss Jerrold Everybody at *Respite* is happy, Mrs Harris.
Fleur That's why we're leaving *Respite*. Not tomorrow. Now. I'm going to pack.
Alice What about your tea?
Fleur Tea can wait. I can't.
Miss Jerrold You'll need to see Mrs Meadowsweet before you go.
Fleur I'll burn that bridge when I come to it.

Fleur hurries out through the archway

Miss Jerrold Your sister is a most impetuous person, Miss Benson.
Alice Martin? Martin? Odd. Very odd. Who was Martin?

Puzzled, Alice wanders out through the french windows

Miss Jerrold Miss Benson, you haven't touched your tea. (*She pours her own. It is very weak*)

You may be right. Something very odd seems to be happening in the kitchen.

The Lights fade to denote the passage to time

Pause. Miss Jerrold exits

Lights up

Miss Brazenose is sitting with her back to the audience, totally immobile

Fleur enters through the archway, carrying a case. She pauses on seeing Miss Brazenose.

Fleur Oh, Miss ... Miss? (*She moves into the room*)

There is no movement from Miss Brazenose not even a flicker of recognition

Are you ill? Is anyone looking after you? Ah! You've been talking to Mrs Meadowsweet again, haven't you? Well, *I'm* talking to you now. I want to know what happened.

Mrs Meadowsweet enters through the french windows

Mrs Meadowsweet Most unfortunate, my dear. (*She moves into the room*) But, I'm afraid inevitable. She was very disturbed. Unhappy memory after unhappy memory.

Fleur And once anybody gives you a memory, it's gone. I've worked out that much.

Mrs Meadowsweet We went back and back until there was nothing left.

Fleur How do you do it?

Mrs Meadowsweet Does that matter, my dear?

Fleur Not to her.

Mrs Meadowsweet Tell me, my dear, when did you ...?

Fleur I mustn't talk to you. I mustn't.

Mrs Meadowsweet Now what have you done to make you so frightened?

Fleur What have *I* done? What have *you* done?

Mrs Meadowsweet I make everybody happy, my dear. Haven't you seen them? All happier than they've been since they were young and innocent. Now why don't you confide in me? You'll find it's like slipping into a warm bath and letting the wickedness of the world wash away.

Fleur And when so much has been washed away that you can't say for certain who you are or how you got here, you can always dig the garden or help in the kitchen. Very useful when there's a guest house to run.

Mrs Meadowsweet Go on, my dear.

Fleur What?

Mrs Meadowsweet You were telling me?

Fleur No.

Mrs Meadowsweet No?

Fleur Whatever I've told you already was too much. I'm not telling you any more. Not knowing what you can do. It all fits. "My name is Inga." That girl in a fuddled haze. All she knows is her name—if she knows even that much by now.

Mrs Meadowsweet No, my dear.

Fleur Where has she gone?

Mrs Meadowsweet She'll rest comfortable under the celery.

Fleur gives a little cry

Don't be afraid of that, my dear. All come to it—cock robin *and* sparrow with his little arrow.

Fleur I saw the hole.

Mrs Meadowsweet Never think of them as holes, my dear. More as beds. But remembering Inga upsets you, does it?

Fleur What do you expect?

Mrs Meadowsweet I shouldn't let it worry me if I were you. As far as you are concerned there never was an Inga. Now—does that make you feel better?

Fleur What do you mean—make me feel better?

Mrs Meadowsweet Not knowing about Inga.

Fleur Inga? I don't know who Inga may have been, but I know who Alice is. At least I know what she was. You're telling me that you make a habit of turning normal human beings . . .

Mrs Meadowsweet Unhappy, twisted, mixed-up beings, my dear.

Fleur All right—turning everyday neurotics into happy zombies.

Mrs Meadowsweet If you like to put it that way, my dear.

Fleur I just did.

Mrs Meadowsweet Very well. I accept the way you put it.

Fleur Your waitress here. Will she disappear now?

Mrs Meadowsweet If you're still afraid of me, there must be some nastiness we haven't got at yet.

Fleur Why do you do it?

Mrs Meadowsweet Kindness, my dear. Simple kindness.

Fleur You kill people. You take away everything that makes them what they are.

Mrs Meadowsweet Only the bad bits.

Fleur The badness is part of us all. Take it away and we're done for.

Mrs Meadowsweet I don't quite follow. Do go on, my dear.
Fleur Yes, I can remember stealing and letting Alice get punished
  for it . . .
Mrs Meadowsweet Go on.
Fleur I can remember doing things I shouldn't have done behind
  the bicycle shed and blush to think of it . . .
Mrs Meadowsweet Don't stop.
Fleur Yes, I can remember worse than that—hurts and disap-
  pointments and bitterness . . .
Mrs Meadowsweet Tell it all.
Fleur But without them I'm a nothing. I'm . . .

The Lights fade

Pause

Lights up

*Fleur, standing with her back to the audience, is now as immobile as
Miss Brazenose*

Mrs Meadowsweet There, my dear. At least your mind's at rest.
  Just put down that case.

*Mrs Meadowsweet tries to take the case but Fleur's fingers seem to
have set round the handle*

You don't have to grasp so tightly, my dear. Perhaps you should
have put it down before you started to look back so far. A pity
this had to happen in such a rush. You had so little time to be
happy. Well, if you won't let go, it must lie in the celery trench
with you.

  Alice enters through the french windows

Alice No! (*She moves into the room*)
Mrs Meadowsweet Were you listening outside, my dear? What did
  you hear? What did you see?
Alice You don't catch me that way again. She gave you every-
  thing, didn't she? Now she's blanked out. Just like Miss
  Brazenose there. And Inga.
Mrs Meadowsweet Inga? You remember Inga?
Alice Fleur did. She told us about her.
Mrs Meadowsweet She told you about Inga, did she? And that
  upset you. Just what did she tell you about Inga?

Alice About who?

Mrs Meadowsweet Are you sure this is your sister? What can you tell me about her?

Alice I know what you're trying to do. You're trying to wipe out Fleur. You'll never make me forget her. You won't. And you'll let her go.

Mrs Meadowsweet Go where, my dear? Can you remember where you are going? Where you come from? Who you really are? All that happened to you from the earliest times to the present day?

Alice I can remember all I want to.

Mrs Meadowsweet (*wincing*) A little lie, but let it pass. After all the lies are used up we are left with the truth. In fact it becomes a relief to let the truth out, my dear. Your sister told you all about me, did she?

Alice No.

Mrs Meadowsweet (*wincing*) That means yes. You were always quarrelling with your sister, weren't you?

Alice No.

Mrs Meadowsweet (*wincing*) Untruths go straight through me, but I suffer in a good cause. Your sister was always made more of than you—being so much younger. You were the centre of attraction until she came, then you never were again. Remember the day you were first told that you had a sister?

Alice I won't. I mean, it wasn't like that at all.

Mrs Meadowsweet How was it then, my dear?

Alice As a matter of fact I was so glad when she came I did a dance on top of the piano.

Mrs Meadowsweet Don't be absurd.

Alice I was a lovely little dancer in those days—classical and modern.

Mrs Meadowsweet (*wincing*) Ah! You're hurting.

Alice I was encouraged by my Uncle Joe—the comic, you know: "Jolly Joe Benson—Game for a Laugh". Did a stand-up turn dressed as a pheasant. He gave up a steady job in the corkscrew works to go on the stage.

Mrs Meadowsweet (*gasping*) A lie's like a knife.

Alice Once you get the stage in your blood you can't get it out. It got in mine from an early age.

Mrs Meadowsweet Stop it before I'm sick.

Alice When I grew up I was going to join my Uncle Joe—as a grouse chick. Then Fleur came along. Jealous? Don't be silly.

We were a double act from the start. She was to be the other half of "The Benson Sisters—Two Twinkling Tots".
Mrs Meadowsweet (*with a hand to her throat*) Aaaah!
Alice Before she could crawl, we were singing duets; and by the time she could stand on her own two feet they were tapping like a trouper's.

Choking, Mrs Meadowsweet staggers towards the archway. Alice follows her, still keeping up the flow of nonsense

We shared the limelight all the way to the top; and we shared everything else when we got there. We couldn't have been closer if we'd been siamese twins. We shone together. Fleur and Alice Benson—The Inseparables!

Slowly Mrs Meadowsweet sinks to her knees, then crumples and lies still. There is a pause

Mrs Meadowsweet?

Silence

What a pity it couldn't really have been like that. Oh, Lord! Now the memory's coming back. Lies hurt you, do they, Mrs Meadowsweet? The truth hurts me. (*She kneels by Mrs Meadowsweet*)
Fleur (*looking round*) Mrs—? Where is she?
Alice Here. Something like a stroke. I think she's ...
Fleur What happens now?
Miss Brazenose (*standing up*) Where is tea? Not ready yet? Really the service in this establishment gets worse.

Mrs Brazenose exits to the garden indignantly

Outside the french windows quarrelling voices can be heard. They could be Miss Jerrold and Inga, but as they are both talking at the same time it hardly matters

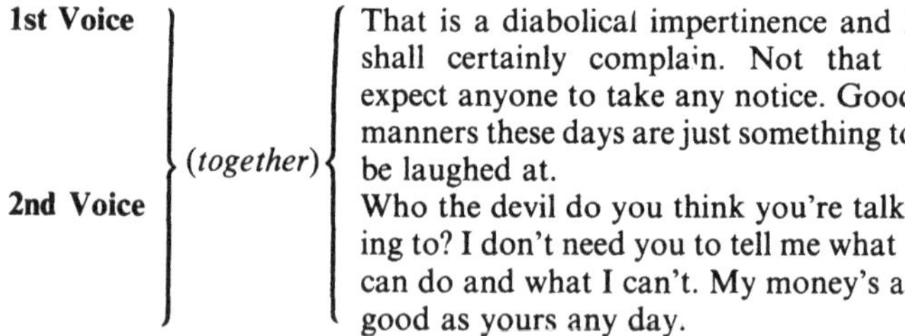

1st Voice		That is a diabolical impertinence and I shall certainly complain. Not that I expect anyone to take any notice. Good manners these days are just something to be laughed at.
	(*together*)	
2nd Voice		Who the devil do you think you're talking to? I don't need you to tell me what I can do and what I can't. My money's as good as yours any day.

The voices move on, still arguing

Alice All over here—for better or worse.
Fleur But which is which?
Alice You have to make your own mind up about that.

CURTAIN

FURNITURE AND PROPERTY LIST

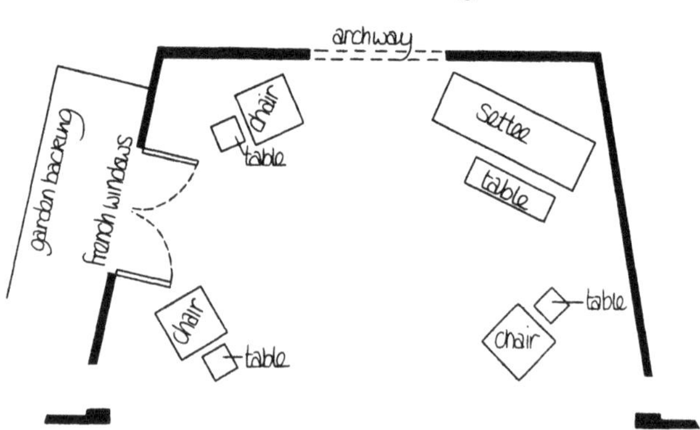

On stage: Several easy chairs
Settee
Small table near the french windows
Several low tables. *On them:* Afternoon tea

Off stage: Tray. *On it:* afternoon tea **(Inga)**
Tray. *On it:* afternoon tea **(Miss Brazenose)**
Suitcase **(Fleur)**

LIGHTING PLOT

Interior. The same scene throughout

Afternoon

To open: General lighting

Cue 1	**Alice:** "... Shall I pour?" *Light fade to Black-out*	(Page 10)
Cue 2	After **Fleur** exits *Lights up*	(Page 10)
Cue 3	**Miss Jerrold:** "... be happening in the kitchen." *Lights fade to Black-out*	(Page 17)
Cue 4	Pause. **Miss Jerrold** exits *Lights up*	(Page 17)
Cue 5	**Fleur:** "But without them I'm nothing. I'm ..." *Lights fade to Black-out*	(Page 20)
Cue 6	Pause *Lights up*	(Page 20)

EFFECTS PLOT

Cue 1	**Miss Jerrold:** "At peace with ..." *Door slams*	(Page 2)

MADE AND PRINTED IN GREAT BRITAIN BY
LATIMER TREND & COMPANY LTD, PLYMOUTH
MADE IN ENGLAND